Welcome to the Jamaican Sl
Ultimate Guide to Speaking

Ever wondered how to naviga.
without accidentally starting a dance-off or mistaking a compliment for a challenge? Fear not! This guide is your ultimate survival kit in the vibrant and rhythm-infused world of Jamaican slang.

Picture this: You're at a Jamaican party, and someone shouts, "Wah gwaan mi yute?" If you're caught staring like a lost tourist, don't worry—we've got you covered. This dictionary will turn you from a clueless bystander into a "vibed-up" expert in no time.

We've packed this book with all the slang you'll need to blend in like a true local. From the sophisticated "zesty" to the perfectly "zooted," and everything in between, we've got phrases that will make you laugh, dance, and maybe even question your life choices.

So, strap in and get ready to dive into a world where "upful" doesn't just mean "cheerful," and where "bad" is, well, really good. Whether you're looking to impress your Jamaican friends or just add a little spice to your vocabulary, this book is your passport to a whole new way of speaking.

Warning: Use of these phrases may result in spontaneous bouts of dancing, sudden cravings for jerk chicken, and an irresistible urge to say "Mi deh yah" with serious conviction.

Now let's get "wicked" with it!

Where is your next travel ?

SCAN THE QR

Get the Slang Dictionary Collection

Slang Dictionaries Availables:

- French
- Italian
- Mexican
- Colombian
- German
- Many More...

TABLE OF CONTENT

A

A weh yuh deh?
Example: "A weh yuh deh, mi a call yuh from mawning!"
Translation: "Where are you? I've been calling you since morning!"

Ackee
Example: "Mi love ackee an' saltfish fi breakfast."
Translation: "I love ackee and saltfish for breakfast."

All fruits ripe
Example: "The party tun up, all fruits ripe now!"
Translation: "The party is in full swing, everything's happening!"

A yaad
Example: "Mi a go stay a yaad today."
Translation: "I'm going to stay home today."

All di while
Example: "Yuh a chat too much all di while."
Translation: "You talk too much all the time."

A go
Example: "Mi a go market later."
Translation: "I'm going to the market later."

A wah?
Example: "A wah yuh a seh?"
Translation: "What are you saying?"

Above mi head
Example: "Di reasoning deh above mi head."
Translation: "That reasoning is beyond my understanding."

A look
Example: "Mi jus a look what gwaan."
Translation: "I'm just observing what's happening."

A wha mi duh?
Example: "A wha mi duh mek yuh vex?"
Translation: "What did I do to make you angry?"

Anansi story
Example: "Nuh badda tell mi no Anansi story."
Translation: "Don't tell me any tall tales."

A gwaan
Example: "Wha gwaan a di dancehall?"
Translation: "What's happening at the dancehall?"

A suh it go
Example: "Mi lose di game, but a suh it go."
Translation: "I lost the game, but that's just how it is."

A go suh
Example: "It nuh really go suh."
Translation: "It didn't really happen like that."

All when
Example: "All when yuh tired, yuh haffi push through."
Translation: "Even when you're tired, you have to push through."

A nuh nutten

Example: "A nuh nutten fi mi do it again."

Translation: "It's nothing for me to do it again."

A long time mi nuh see yuh

Example: "A long time mi nuh see yuh, wah gwaan?"

Translation: "It's been a while since I saw you, how are things?"

All bout

Example: "Mi look fi di book all bout."

Translation: "I searched everywhere for the book."

A true

Example: "A true yuh a talk, mi agree."

Translation: "You're speaking the truth, I agree."

All when

Example: "All when yuh wrong, mi still a support yuh."

Translation: "Even when you're wrong, I'll still support you."

B

Bashment
Example: "Di bashment party did mad!"
Translation: "The party was amazing!"

Big up
Example: "Big up yuhself, mi fren."
Translation: "Respect yourself, my friend."

Bredren
Example: "Mi bredren an mi guh out last night."
Translation: "My friend and I went out last night."

Boasy
Example: "Di yute deh too boasy."
Translation: "That guy is too boastful."

Bwoy
Example: "Bwoy, yuh nuh easy."
Translation: "Boy, you're something else."

Bun
Example: "Di bread bun up inna di oven."
Translation: "The bread got burnt in the oven."

Bickle
Example: "Mi have some bickle fi yuh."
Translation: "I have some food for you."

Brawta
Example: "Mi buy two mango an di man gimme a brawta."

Translation: "I bought two mangoes and the man gave me an extra one."

Bun mi
Example: "Yuh words bun mi deep."
Translation: "Your words hurt me deeply."

Big up di ting
Example: "Wi haffi big up di ting pon social media."
Translation: "We have to promote it on social media."

Bex
Example: "Mi nuh know why yuh bex wid mi."
Translation: "I don't know why you're upset with me."

Bad man
Example: "Him a real bad man."
Translation: "He's a real tough guy."

Bun fi bun
Example: "Him gi mi bun, so mi gi him bun fi bun."
Translation: "He cheated on me, so I cheated on him too."

Bright
Example: "Yuh too bright fi yuh age."
Translation: "You're too forward for your age."

Buss a move
Example: "Di DJ buss a move an di crowd love it."
Translation: "The DJ made a move and the crowd loved it."

Bagga mout
Example: "Di woman deh a bagga mout."

Translation: "That woman is too talkative."

Bun dung
Example: "Di house bun dung completely."
Translation: "The house burnt down completely."

Bruck out
Example: "Di gal dem bruck out at di party."
Translation: "The girls danced wildly at the party."

Brawlin
Example: "Dem start fight brawlin inna di street."
Translation: "They started fighting openly in the street."

Baff
Example: "Mi haffi go tek a baff before mi go out."
Translation: "I need to take a bath before I go out."

C

Cyaah badda
Example: "Mi cyaah badda wid di stress."
Translation: "I can't be bothered with the stress."

Chatty chatty
Example: "Di man too chatty chatty."
Translation: "The man is too talkative."

Criss
Example: "Di car criss an clean."
Translation: "The car is nice and clean."

Cutchie
Example: "Wi a pass di cutchie roun' di corner."
Translation: "We're passing the smoking pipe around the corner."

Claat
Example: "Mi naw go tek no claat from dem."
Translation: "I'm not going to take any nonsense from them."

Cyaan
Example: "Mi cyaan believe yuh did dat."
Translation: "I can't believe you did that."

Cut eye
Example: "She cut eye pon mi when she see mi."
Translation: "She gave me a dirty look when she saw me."

Cyaan tan
Example: "Mi cyaan tan deh suh no longer."
Translation: "I can't stand being there any longer."

Claat up
Example: "Di man get claat up by di police."
Translation: "The man got beaten by the police."

Clean
Example: "Yuh outfit clean, mi rate it."
Translation: "Your outfit is stylish, I like it."

Cuss cuss
Example: "Dem deh pan cuss cuss all day."
Translation: "They were arguing all day."

Cut an go tru
Example: "Yuh fi cut an go tru quietly."
Translation: "You should leave quietly."

Craven
Example: "Di yute craven, him eat off all di food."
Translation: "The guy is greedy, he ate all the food."

Catch di light
Example: "Di driver catch di light just in time."
Translation: "The driver made it through the traffic light just in time."

Cyaan bodda
Example: "Mi cyaan bodda wid di foolishness."
Translation: "I can't be bothered with the foolishness."

Cut mi eye
Example: "She cut mi eye an walk weh."
Translation: "She gave me a dirty look and walked away."

Cool nuh
Example: "Cool nuh, mi a sort it out."
Translation: "Calm down, I'm handling it."

Cyaan done
Example: "Di food cyaan done, it nuff."
Translation: "The food can't run out, there's plenty."

Caw
Example: "Caw yuh nuh listen, yuh get inna trouble."
Translation: "Because you didn't listen, you got into trouble."

Cyaah cross it
Example: "Di river too high, cyaah cross it."
Translation: "The river is too high, I can't cross it."

D

Dat
Example: "Dat mi a talk bout!"
Translation: "That's what I'm talking about!"

Deh yah
Example: "Mi just deh yah, chillin'."
Translation: "I'm just here, chilling."

Dutty
Example: "Di shoes dutty up."
Translation: "The shoes got dirty."

Dis yah one
Example: "Dis yah one yah different."
Translation: "This one is different."

Draw fi
Example: "Di bwoy draw fi him knife."
Translation: "The boy pulled out his knife."

Done
Example: "Di food done already?"
Translation: "Is the food finished already?"

Dun know
Example: "Yuh dun know mi a roll out tonight."
Translation: "You already know I'm going out tonight."

Dis yah time
Example: "Dis yah time, mi ago win."
Translation: "This time, I'm going to win."

Drop a sleep
Example: "Mi drop a sleep pon di bus."
Translation: "I fell asleep on the bus."

Dweet
Example: "If yuh wah do it, just dweet!"
Translation: "If you want to do it, just do it!"

Di tings
Example: "Mi have di tings dem ready."
Translation: "I have the things ready."

Dawg
Example: "Mi dawg, wha gwaan?"
Translation: "My friend, what's going on?"

Dem deh
Example: "Dem deh shoes mi naw wear."
Translation: "I'm not wearing those shoes."

Drop out
Example: "Di old man drop out last night."
Translation: "The old man passed away last night."

Dutty wine
Example: "Di girl dem a do di dutty wine."
Translation: "The girls are doing the dirty wine dance."

Dis yah man
Example: "Dis yah man nuh easy."
Translation: "This man isn't easy to deal with."

Dash weh
Example: "Di food spoil, mi affi dash it weh."
Translation: "The food spoiled, I had to throw it away."

Dem a watch
Example: "Dem a watch mi every move."
Translation: "They're watching my every move."

Di real ting
Example: "Dis yah di real ting, nuh fake."
Translation: "This is the real deal, not fake."

Deh pon
Example: "Mi deh pon di phone all night."
Translation: "I was on the phone all night."

E

Eh-heh
Example: "Eh-heh, mi neva know dat!"
Translation: "Oh really, I didn't know that!"

Ease up
Example: "Ease up pon di speed."
Translation: "Slow down a bit."

Eena
Example: "Mi eena di house a rest."
Translation: "I'm inside the house resting."

Engage
Example: "Di gyal engage mi inna di conversation."
Translation: "The girl engaged me in the conversation."

Eh?
Example: "Yuh really believe dat, eh?"
Translation: "You really believe that, huh?"

Excuse mi
Example: "Excuse mi, mi need fi pass."
Translation: "Excuse me, I need to pass."

Eyewata
Example: "Di fight bring eyewata to mi eyes."
Translation: "The fight brought tears to my eyes."

Every mickle mek a muckle
Example: "Save yuh money, every mickle mek a muckle."
Translation: "Save your money, every little bit adds up."

Exhibit A
Example: "Yuh late again, exhibit A why mi nuh trus' yuh."
Translation: "You're late again, here's proof why I don't trust you."

Ease off
Example: "Mi haffi ease off di drinkin'."
Translation: "I have to cut back on drinking."

Eh nuh
Example: "Di food nice, eh nuh?"
Translation: "The food is good, isn't it?"

Entertain
Example: "Wi a entertain some guests later."
Translation: "We're hosting some guests later."

Eediat ting
Example: "Mi nah tek part inna no eediat ting."
Translation: "I'm not participating in any foolishness."

Elevate
Example: "Wi need fi elevate wi mindset."
Translation: "We need to elevate our mindset."

Everyting crisp
Example: "Everyting crisp, nuh worry."
Translation: "Everything's good, don't worry."

Ease di tension
Example: "Music a play fi ease di tension."
Translation: "Music is playing to ease the tension."

Eat mi outta house an home
Example: "Di pickney dem eat mi outta house an home."
Translation: "The kids ate all my food."

Ever bless
Example: "Mi deh yah, ever bless."
Translation: "I'm here, always blessed."

Express yuhself
Example: "Nuh badda shy, express yuhself."
Translation: "Don't be shy, express yourself."

Ease di pain
Example: "Mi tek some tea fi ease di pain."
Translation: "I had some tea to ease the pain."

F

Fawud
Example: "Mi a fawud to di party later."
Translation: "I'm coming to the party later."

Fi real
Example: "Yuh seh so? Fi real?"
Translation: "You said that? Really?"

Fren
Example: "Mi fren dem loyal."
Translation: "My friends are loyal."

Frass
Example: "Di man look frass outta di dance."
Translation: "The man looked worn out after the dance."

Fish
Example: "Di man love fish, him nyam it every day."
Translation: "The man loves fish, he eats it every day."

Fi wi
Example: "Di house a fi wi."
Translation: "The house is ours."

Feisty
Example: "Yuh likkle gal, yuh too feisty!"
Translation: "You little girl, you're too rude!"

Fyah bun
Example: "Fyah bun all hypocrite!"
Translation: "Curse all hypocrites!"

Flim
Example: "Wi a watch flim later."
Translation: "We're watching a movie later."

Fiya fi dat
Example: "Fiya fi dat man weh tell lie."
Translation: "Shame on that man who tells lies."

Flex
Example: "Mi a flex wid mi bredren dem tonight."
Translation: "I'm hanging out with my friends tonight."

Fling weh
Example: "Di man fling weh di old shoes."
Translation: "The man threw away the old shoes."

Falla
Example: "Nuh falla bad company."
Translation: "Don't follow bad company."

Fi chue
Example: "Yuh fi chue, mi agree wid yuh."
Translation: "You're right, I agree with you."

Fass
Example: "Di neighbor dem too fass inna mi business."
Translation: "The neighbors are too nosy in my business."

Fah real
Example: "Yuh a seh dat fah real?"
Translation: "Are you saying that for real?"

Firm
Example: "Yuh haffi firm up an face yuh problems."
Translation: "You have to stand strong and face your problems."

Fast track
Example: "Di DJ a fast track di tune dem."
Translation: "The DJ is quickly playing the tunes."

Fling stone
Example: "Di bwoy fling stone an mash up di glass."
Translation: "The boy threw a stone and broke the glass."

Falla fashion
Example: "Yuh too falla fashion, be yuhself."
Translation: "You're too much of a follower, be yourself."

G

Gwaan
Example: "Yuh can gwaan talk, mi nah listen."
Translation: "You can keep talking, I'm not listening."

Galang
Example: "Galang good, mi fren."
Translation: "Take care, my friend."

Gyal
Example: "Di gyal dem out inna di place."
Translation: "The girls are out in the place."

Guh tru
Example: "Mi see yuh, guh tru mi yute."
Translation: "I see you, go ahead, my friend."

Guh deh
Example: "Guh deh, yuh a do yuh ting."
Translation: "Go on, you're doing your thing."

Grave
Example: "Di man voice grave, it deep."
Translation: "The man's voice is deep."

Gyal clown
Example: "Di bwoy a gyal clown, him do anything fi har."
Translation: "The boy is a fool for the girl, he'll do anything for her."

Gimme a bly
Example: "Gimme a bly, mi late fi work."

Translation: "Give me a pass, I'm late for work."

Gi trouble
Example: "Di pickney dem gi trouble when dem bored."
Translation: "The children cause trouble when they're bored."

Gwaan bad
Example: "Di DJ did a gwaan bad las' night."
Translation: "The DJ was performing exceptionally well last night."

Gi mi likkle space
Example: "Gi mi likkle space fi pass."
Translation: "Give me some space to pass."

Goodas
Example: "She a real goodas, always well put together."
Translation: "She's a real classy lady, always well put together."

Gully
Example: "Di yute dem a run di gully side."
Translation: "The youth are controlling the rough area."

Gal pal
Example: "Mi gal pal an mi a guh out lata."
Translation: "My girlfriend and I are going out later."

Get a buss
Example: "Di artist get a buss pon di radio."
Translation: "The artist got a break on the radio."

Gwaan easy
Example: "Just gwaan easy an relax."
Translation: "Just take it easy and relax."

Gi dem chat
Example: "She gi dem chat, mek dem know how she feel."
Translation: "She told them off, made them know how she feels."

Gwan
Example: "Yuh a gwan like yuh nuh know mi."
Translation: "You're acting like you don't know me."

Get up
Example: "Mi haffi get up early tomorrow."
Translation: "I have to wake up early tomorrow."

Gi mi a chance
Example: "Gi mi a chance fi prove miself."
Translation: "Give me a chance to prove myself."

H

Hush
Example: "Hush, mi nuh mean fi hurt yuh."
Translation: "Sorry, I didn't mean to hurt you."

Hot stepper
Example: "Di man a hot stepper pon di dance floor."
Translation: "The man is a great dancer."

Hype
Example: "Yuh nuh haffi hype up yuhself."
Translation: "You don't need to boast."

Hol' a vibes
Example: "Wi just a hol' a vibes an' chill."
Translation: "We're just having a good time and relaxing."

Hot gal
Example: "She a real hot gal, always lookin' good."
Translation: "She's a real attractive girl, always looking good."

Hol' di faith
Example: "Mi a try hol' di faith despite di struggles."
Translation: "I'm trying to keep the faith despite the struggles."

Heng out
Example: "Wi a heng out pon di corner."
Translation: "We're hanging out on the corner."

Hot head

Example: "Di bwoy a hot head, him quick fi get vex."
Translation: "The boy has a temper, he's quick to get angry."

Heng up
Example: "Mi heng up di phone when mi done talk."
Translation: "I hung up the phone when I finished talking."

Hot like fyah
Example: "Di soup hot like fyah, careful!"
Translation: "The soup is extremely hot, be careful!"

Haf fi
Example: "Mi haf fi do it now or else."
Translation: "I have to do it now, or else."

High grade
Example: "Di man always a smoke high grade."
Translation: "The man always smokes the best marijuana."

Hot minute
Example: "Mi nuh see yuh from a hot minute."
Translation: "I haven't seen you in a while."

Haffi mek it
Example: "No matter what, mi haffi mek it in life."
Translation: "No matter what, I have to succeed in life."

Humble yuhself
Example: "Yuh need fi humble yuhself, yuh too hype."
Translation: "You need to humble yourself, you're too boastful."

Hol' tight
Example: "Mi deh yah, hol' tight."
Translation: "I'm here, stay strong."

Heart clean
Example: "Di man heart clean, him nuh have nuh bad mind."
Translation: "The man has a good heart, he's not envious."

Hustle hard
Example: "Wi haffi hustle hard fi mek ends meet."
Translation: "We have to work hard to make a living."

Hol' di vibes
Example: "Wi deh yah fi hol' di vibes an enjoy wi self."
Translation: "We're here to enjoy the vibes and have a good time."

Hitch up
Example: "Di man hitch up pon di corner a chat."
Translation: "The man is hanging out on the corner, chatting."

I

Inna
Example: "Mi inna di house all day."
Translation: "I've been in the house all day."

Informa
Example: "Nobody nuh like a informa inna di group."
Translation: "Nobody likes a snitch in the group."

Irie
Example: "Everything irie, nuh worries."
Translation: "Everything's fine, no worries."

Ital
Example: "Mi a eat ital food fi di week."
Translation: "I'm eating vegetarian food for the week."

Inna di dance
Example: "Wi a guh inna di dance tonight."
Translation: "We're going to the dance tonight."

Inna yuh feelings
Example: "Yuh inna yuh feelings ova di argument."
Translation: "You're emotional over the argument."

Inna mi head
Example: "Mi deh yah a think, it inna mi head."
Translation: "I'm here thinking, it's on my mind."

Island vibes
Example: "Di island vibes sweet, mi nah lie."
Translation: "The island vibes are nice, I'm not lying."

Inna di works
Example: "Di new project inna di works."
Translation: "The new project is in progress."

Inna dem skin
Example: "Di girl dem deh inna dem skin tonight."
Translation: "The girls are looking good tonight."

Inna di street
Example: "Mi bredren deh inna di street daily."
Translation: "My friend is out in the streets daily."

It bun mi
Example: "When mi lose di game, it bun mi."
Translation: "When I lost the game, it hurt me."

Ites
Example: "Di Rastaman love di ites food."
Translation: "The Rastaman loves vegetarian food."

Inna di light
Example: "Di truth come out inna di light."
Translation: "The truth came out in the open."

Inna di miggle
Example: "Wi inna di miggle of di argument."
Translation: "We're in the middle of the argument."

Inna di mood
Example: "Mi inna di mood fi some music."
Translation: "I'm in the mood for some music."

Inna mi shoes
Example: "If yuh did inna mi shoes, yuh woulda understand."
Translation: "If you were in my shoes, you would understand."

Inna mi own lane
Example: "Mi jus' a stay inna mi own lane."
Translation: "I'm just staying in my own lane."

Inna di party
Example: "Di crew inna di party fi real."
Translation: "The crew is really in the party."

Inna di morning
Example: "Mi a wake up early inna di morning."
Translation: "I'm waking up early in the morning."

J

Jah know
Example: "Jah know, di food taste good."
Translation: "God knows, the food tastes good."

Jah bless
Example: "Jah bless mi wid health an' strength."
Translation: "God has blessed me with health and strength."

Jus' cool
Example: "Mi jus' cool, nuh stress."
Translation: "I'm just relaxing, no stress."

Jook
Example: "Di pin jook mi hand."
Translation: "The pin pricked my hand."

Jus' deh yah
Example: "Mi jus' deh yah a hol' a vibes."
Translation: "I'm just here chilling."

Jamrock
Example: "Welcome to Jamrock, land of reggae."
Translation: "Welcome to Jamaica, land of reggae."

Jacket
Example: "Di baby look like a jacket, nuh look like him father."
Translation: "The baby doesn't resemble his supposed father."

Jus' a go tru

Example: "Mi jus' a go tru some tings right now."

Translation: "I'm just going through some things right now."

Jah guide

Example: "Jah guide mi pon di journey."

Translation: "God guide me on the journey."

Jus' reach

Example: "Mi jus' reach a di party."

Translation: "I just arrived at the party."

Jus' a pass tru

Example: "Mi jus' a pass tru di town."

Translation: "I'm just passing through the town."

Jus' a chill

Example: "Wi jus' a chill pon di ends."

Translation: "We're just hanging out in the area."

Jus' gwaan

Example: "Jus' gwaan do yuh ting."

Translation: "Just keep doing your thing."

Jus' a vibe

Example: "Mi jus' a vibe to di music."

Translation: "I'm just vibing to the music."

Jus' a pree

Example: "Mi jus' a pree di situation."

Translation: "I'm just observing the situation."

Jah light
Example: "Mi follow Jah light inna di dark times."
Translation: "I follow God's guidance in dark times."

Jah works
Example: "Mi a do Jah works every day."
Translation: "I'm doing God's work every day."

Jah ras
Example: "Jah ras! Di man brave!"
Translation: "Oh my God! The man is brave!"

Jus' a gwaan
Example: "Mi jus' a gwaan do mi work."
Translation: "I'm just continuing with my work."

Jump up
Example: "Di crowd jump up when di music start."
Translation: "The crowd jumped up when the music started."

K

Ketch up
Example: "Di two man dem ketch up ova a small ting."
Translation: "The two men got into an argument over a small issue."

Kotch
Example: "Mi just kotch a di corner fi now."
Translation: "I'm just hanging out at the corner for now."

Kaya
Example: "Mi a bun some kaya tonight."
Translation: "I'm smoking some marijuana tonight."

Kick up
Example: "Di horse kick up plenty dust."
Translation: "The horse stirred up a lot of dust."

Klassy
Example: "She always dress klassy when she go out."
Translation: "She always dresses classy when she goes out."

Krun
Example: "Di man krun di car roun' di corner."
Translation: "The man turned the car around the corner quickly."

Ketchy shuby
Example: "Di dance was full a ketchy shuby vibes."
Translation: "The dance was full of energetic and close dancing."

Killa
Example: "Mi killa, how yuh a do?"
Translation: "My friend, how are you doing?"

Knock pon
Example: "Mi knock pon di door, but nobody neva answer."
Translation: "I knocked on the door, but no one answered."

Killa bee
Example: "Di killa bee crew a run di place."
Translation: "The tough crew is dominating the area."

Kick back
Example: "Mi a go kick back an' watch a movie."
Translation: "I'm going to relax and watch a movie."

Kumina
Example: "Di kumina dance deep inna tradition."
Translation: "The Kumina dance is deeply rooted in tradition."

Ketch yuh style
Example: "Mi ketch yuh style, yuh a gwaan good."
Translation: "I notice your style, you're doing well."

Kibba yuh mouth
Example: "Kibba yuh mouth, nuh talk so much."
Translation: "Keep your mouth shut, don't talk so much."

Kick off
Example: "Di party a go kick off at 10 o'clock."
Translation: "The party will start at 10 o'clock."

Kotch up
Example: "She kotch up beside mi pon di sofa."
Translation: "She sat close to me on the sofa."

Krun fi run
Example: "Yuh haffi krun fi run inna dis world."
Translation: "You have to be sharp to survive in this world."

Ketch di beat
Example: "Di dancer ketch di beat real quick."
Translation: "The dancer caught the rhythm really quickly."

Kick start
Example: "Wi need fi kick start di project soon."
Translation: "We need to start the project soon."

Kool fi now
Example: "Mi a go kool fi now an' tek it easy."
Translation: "I'm going to take it easy for now."

L

Likkle more
Example: "Mi a see yuh likkle more."
Translation: "I'll see you later."

Likkle bit
Example: "Mi only have likkle bit a money lef'."
Translation: "I only have a little bit of money left."

Labrish
Example: "Dem deh pon di corna a labrish all day."
Translation: "They're gossiping on the corner all day."

Link up
Example: "Wi a go link up lata."
Translation: "We're going to meet up later."

Leggo
Example: "Leggo mi hand, mi a go now."
Translation: "Let go of my hand, I'm leaving now."

Low mi
Example: "Low mi, mi nuh inna di mood fi chat."
Translation: "Leave me alone, I'm not in the mood to talk."

Likkle more time
Example: "Gimme likkle more time fi finish di work."
Translation: "Give me a little more time to finish the work."

Look yah
Example: "Look yah, di place nice!"

Translation: "Look here, the place is nice!"

Lively up
Example: "Di DJ a lively up di dance."
Translation: "The DJ is energizing the party."

Livity
Example: "Di livity of di people dem strong."
Translation: "The energy of the people is strong."

Likkle miss
Example: "Likkle miss always deh pon time."
Translation: "The young girl is always on time."

Long time
Example: "Mi nuh see yuh from long time."
Translation: "I haven't seen you in a long time."

Likkle more den
Example: "Mi talk to yuh likkle more den."
Translation: "I'll talk to you later, then."

Loud up
Example: "Di bwoy loud up mi name inna di place."
Translation: "The boy is talking about me loudly in the place."

Lean pon
Example: "Mi can always lean pon mi fren fi support."
Translation: "I can always rely on my friend for support."

Lock down
Example: "Di police lock down di party early."

Translation: "The police shut down the party early."

Likkle bwoy
Example: "Yuh a act like a likkle bwoy, grow up."
Translation: "You're acting like a little boy, grow up."

Low yuh ting
Example: "Low yuh ting an focus pon di bigger picture."
Translation: "Leave your petty issues and focus on the bigger picture."

Lick out
Example: "Di box lick out mi tooth."
Translation: "The punch knocked out my tooth."

Long reach
Example: "Mi haffi mek a long reach fi di job."
Translation: "I have to travel a long distance for the job."

M

Mi deh yah
Example: "Mi deh yah a wait fi yuh."
Translation: "I'm here waiting for you."

Mi soon come
Example: "Mi soon come back fi di bag."
Translation: "I'll be back soon for the bag."

Mi fren
Example: "Mi fren a di best cook."
Translation: "My friend is the best cook."

Mek mi tell yuh
Example: "Mek mi tell yuh something important."
Translation: "Let me tell you something important."

Mi nah lie
Example: "Mi nah lie, di movie was good."
Translation: "I'm not lying, the movie was good."

Mi yard
Example: "Come link mi a mi yard."
Translation: "Come visit me at my home."

Mek wi move
Example: "Mek wi move before it start rain."
Translation: "Let's leave before it starts to rain."

Mek haste
Example: "Mek haste an finish di work."
Translation: "Hurry up and finish the work."

Mi pickney
Example: "Mi pickney dem a go school now."
Translation: "My children are going to school now."

Mi vibes
Example: "Mi vibes nuh right today."
Translation: "I'm not feeling right today."

Mi an yuh
Example: "Mi an yuh need fi talk later."
Translation: "You and I need to talk later."

Mek wi reason
Example: "Mek wi reason out di situation."
Translation: "Let's discuss the situation."

Mek mi explain
Example: "Mek mi explain why mi late."
Translation: "Let me explain why I'm late."

Mi bredda
Example: "Mi bredda always have mi back."
Translation: "My brother always supports me."

Mek wi run
Example: "Mek wi run go di shop quick."
Translation: "Let's quickly go to the shop."

Mi cyaan
Example: "Mi cyaan believe yuh do dat."
Translation: "I can't believe you did that."

Mek mi think
Example: "Mek mi think bout it an' get back to yuh."
Translation: "Let me think about it and get back to you."

Mi ting
Example: "Mi ting well set up now."
Translation: "My situation is well set up now."

Mek mi check
Example: "Mek mi check di time before mi leave."
Translation: "Let me check the time before I leave."

Mi mind
Example: "Mi mind tell mi seh something nuh right."
Translation: "My intuition tells me that something is wrong."

N

Nuff respect
Example: "Nuff respect to di elders."
Translation: "Much respect to the elders."

Nuh problem
Example: "Nuh problem, mi wi deal wid it."
Translation: "No problem, I'll handle it."

Nuh worry yuhself
Example: "Nuh worry yuhself, everything good."
Translation: "Don't worry, everything is fine."

Nuh bodda
Example: "Nuh bodda come if yuh busy."
Translation: "Don't bother coming if you're busy."

Nuh mek sense
Example: "It nuh mek sense argue over it."
Translation: "It doesn't make sense to argue about it."

Nuh watch dat
Example: "Nuh watch dat, mi wi deal wid it."
Translation: "Don't worry about that, I'll handle it."

Nuh long talk
Example: "Nuh long talk, just do di work."
Translation: "No need for a long conversation, just do the work."

Nuh true?
Example: "Yuh see how di place change? Nuh true?"

Translation: "You see how the place has changed? Isn't that right?"

Nuh badda wid dat
Example: "Nuh badda wid dat attitude yah."
Translation: "Don't continue with that attitude."

Nuh easy
Example: "Di man nuh easy at all, him full a tricks."
Translation: "The man is cunning, he's full of tricks."

Nuh watch nuh face
Example: "Just go fi it, nuh watch nuh face."
Translation: "Just go for it, don't worry about what others think."

Nuh tek it serious
Example: "Nuh tek it serious, wi just a joke."
Translation: "Don't take it seriously, we're just joking."

Nuh bad mind
Example: "Nuh bad mind di man fi him success."
Translation: "Don't envy the man for his success."

Nuh see nothing yet
Example: "Yuh nuh see nothing yet, more fi come."
Translation: "You haven't seen anything yet, there's more to come."

Nuh bodda stress
Example: "Nuh bodda stress, tings a go work out."
Translation: "Don't stress, things will work out."

Nuh lick head
Example: "Mi nah nuh lick head, mi a deal wid it."
Translation: "I'm not foolish, I'm handling it."

Nuh gwan so
Example: "Nuh gwan so, yuh too rude."
Translation: "Don't behave like that, you're being too rude."

Nuh rate mi?
Example: "How yuh nuh rate mi, mi always deh fi yuh."
Translation: "How do you not respect me, I'm always there for you."

Nuh far
Example: "Di shop nuh far, wi can walk."
Translation: "The shop isn't far, we can walk."

Nuh dat mi mean
Example: "Nuh dat mi mean, yuh misunderstand mi."
Translation: "That's not what I meant, you misunderstood me."

O

Out deh
Example: "Di man always out deh, nuh time fi rest."
Translation: "The man is always out and about, no time to rest."

Overstand
Example: "Yuh need fi overstand di situation betta."
Translation: "You need to understand the situation better."

Old foot
Example: "Mi a old foot inna di business, mi know di ropes."
Translation: "I'm experienced in the business, I know the ins and outs."

Outta dis
Example: "Mi cyaan deal wid dis, mi outta dis."
Translation: "I can't handle this, I'm out."

On top a tings
Example: "Di man always on top a tings, nuh slip up."
Translation: "The man is always on top of things, no mistakes."

Over mi head
Example: "Di talk go over mi head, mi nuh understand."
Translation: "The conversation went over my head, I didn't understand."

On di case
Example: "Mi on di case, yuh can trust mi."
Translation: "I'm handling it, you can trust me."

One love
Example: "Wi a preach one love to di world."
Translation: "We're promoting unity and love to the world."

Outta mi way
Example: "Move outta mi way, mi a pass."
Translation: "Get out of my way, I'm passing through."

On a level
Example: "Mi need fi talk to yuh on a level."
Translation: "I need to have a serious talk with you."

Over di moon
Example: "Mi over di moon wid joy."
Translation: "I'm extremely happy."

Outta pocket
Example: "Yuh outta pocket fi dat comment."
Translation: "You're out of line for that comment."

Old time something
Example: "Mi love di old time something dem, dem classic."
Translation: "I love the old-fashioned things, they're classic."

On di rise
Example: "Di youth dem on di rise inna di music industry."
Translation: "The young people are making progress in the music industry."

Outta road
Example: "Di news outta road travel fast."
Translation: "The news in the streets travels fast."

On di front line
Example: "Di workers deh pon di front line everyday."
Translation: "The workers are on the front line every day."

Out fi get mi
Example: "Mi feel like somebody out fi get mi."
Translation: "I feel like someone is trying to harm me."

Off di grid
Example: "Di man go off di grid fi a while."
Translation: "The man went off the radar for a while."

Over di top
Example: "Di performance was over di top, mi love it!"
Translation: "The performance was exceptional, I loved it!"

On point
Example: "Di outfit on point, mi nah lie."
Translation: "The outfit is perfect, I'm not lying."

P

Pickney
Example: "Mi pickney dem love fi play inna di yard."
Translation: "My children love to play in the yard."

Pree
Example: "Mi a pree di new car mi waan buy."
Translation: "I'm considering the new car I want to buy."

Patty fi patty
Example: "Wi a trade patty fi patty, mi gi yuh one, yuh gi mi one."
Translation: "We're trading tit for tat, I give you one, you give me one."

Par
Example: "Mi an mi bredda par everyday."
Translation: "My brother and I hang out every day."

Pop dung
Example: "Di old building pop dung last night."
Translation: "The old building collapsed last night."

Pressa
Example: "Di boss a put pressa pon mi fi finish di work."
Translation: "The boss is putting pressure on me to finish the work."

Play yuhself
Example: "Nuh play yuhself, stay focused."
Translation: "Don't mess up, stay focused."

Pumpy
Example: "Him a move like a big pumpy inna di place."
Translation: "He's acting like a big shot in the place."

Puppalick
Example: "Di man deh a move like a puppalick, nuh sense."
Translation: "That man is behaving foolishly, without sense."

Puss n dawg
Example: "Dem two deh a live like puss n dawg, always a fight."
Translation: "Those two live like cat and dog, always fighting."

Push up yuh mout
Example: "Nuh push up yuh mout when mi a talk."
Translation: "Don't pout when I'm talking."

Pass di dutchie
Example: "Pass di dutchie pon di left hand side."
Translation: "Pass the cooking pot (or joint) to the left-hand side."

Pree dem
Example: "Mi a pree dem fi a while, dem look suspicious."
Translation: "I've been watching them for a while, they look suspicious."

Pinky
Example: "Mi gi har di pinky promise fi keep di secret."
Translation: "I made her a pinky promise to keep the secret."

Puff puff pass
Example: "Mi seh puff puff pass, nuh hold on to it too long."
Translation: "I said puff puff pass, don't hold onto it too long."

Push come to shove
Example: "If push come to shove, wi will handle it."
Translation: "If things get tough, we will handle it."

Pon top
Example: "Mi waan mi team pon top a di league."
Translation: "I want my team at the top of the league."

Pree life
Example: "Mi just a pree life an' give thanks."
Translation: "I'm just reflecting on life and giving thanks."

Piece a cake
Example: "Di test was a piece a cake, mi pass it easy."
Translation: "The test was very easy, I passed it effortlessly."

Proper
Example: "Di food proper, mi belly full."
Translation: "The food is great, I'm full."

Q

Quick step
Example: "Mi haffi quick step fi ketch di bus."
Translation: "I had to hurry to catch the bus."

Quiet as a mouse
Example: "Di pickney dem quiet as a mouse when di teacher a talk."
Translation: "The children are very quiet when the teacher is speaking."

Quashie
Example: "Yuh nuh see seh di man a quashie, him nuh know nothing."
Translation: "Can't you see the man is a fool, he doesn't know anything."

Quit yuh noise
Example: "Quit yuh noise an' listen to mi."
Translation: "Stop making noise and listen to me."

Quarrel
Example: "Dem always a quarrel over di small tings."
Translation: "They are always arguing over the smallest things."

Quake
Example: "Di whole place start fi quake when di music drop."
Translation: "The whole place started to shake when the music played."

Quality time
Example: "Mi need fi spend some quality time wid mi family."
Translation: "I need to spend some quality time with my family."

Quitter
Example: "Mi nah no quitter, mi a go finish dis."
Translation: "I'm not a quitter, I'm going to finish this."

Quench yuh thirst
Example: "Come drink some wata fi quench yuh thirst."
Translation: "Come drink some water to quench your thirst."

Quick time
Example: "Wi need fi move quick time if wi want reach early."
Translation: "We need to move quickly if we want to arrive early."

Quench di fire
Example: "Dem try fi quench di fire but it did too strong."
Translation: "They tried to extinguish the fire, but it was too strong."

Quiet spot
Example: "Mi a look fi a quiet spot fi relax."
Translation: "I'm looking for a quiet place to relax."

Quarter to
Example: "Mi a leave quarter to eight, nuh mek mi late."
Translation: "I'm leaving at 7:45, don't make me late."

Quash
Example: "Di judge quash di case, seh dem nuh have no evidence."
Translation: "The judge dismissed the case, saying they had no evidence."

Quick chat
Example: "Mi just waan fi have a quick chat wid yuh."
Translation: "I just want to have a quick conversation with you."

Quintessential
Example: "Him a di quintessential Jamaican, always cool an' calm."
Translation: "He is the perfect example of a Jamaican, always cool and calm."

Quiver
Example: "Mi voice start fi quiver when mi haffi talk to di boss."
Translation: "My voice started to shake when I had to speak to the boss."

Quote unquote
Example: "Him seh quote unquote, mi a di best worker yah."
Translation: "He said, quote unquote, I'm the best worker here."

Quick-fix
Example: "Di repairman gi mi a quick-fix solution fi di problem."

Translation: "The repairman gave me a temporary solution to the problem."

Quarrel wid mi shadow
Example: "Him woulda quarrel wid him shadow, always vex."
Translation: "He would even argue with his shadow, he's always angry."

R

Rude bwoy
Example: "Di rude bwoy dem run di street at night."
Translation: "The tough guys run the street at night."

Raggamuffin
Example: "Di DJ drop a raggamuffin tune."
Translation: "The DJ played a hard-hitting reggae song."

Run tings
Example: "Yuh know seh mi run tings round here."
Translation: "You know that I'm in charge around here."

Ramp rough
Example: "Di yute dem a ramp rough inna di schoolyard."
Translation: "The kids are playing rough in the schoolyard."

Run come
Example: "When dem hear di news, everybody run come."
Translation: "When they heard the news, everyone rushed over."

Rassclaat
Example: "Rassclaat! Mi can't believe it!"
Translation: "Damn! I can't believe it!"

Ready up
Example: "Ready up di place, wi a leave soon."
Translation: "Get everything ready, we're leaving soon."

Rough it out
Example: "Wi haffi rough it out till betta days come."

Translation: "We have to endure until better days come."

Real talk
Example: "Mi nah lie, real talk, yuh di right."
Translation: "I'm not lying, it's the truth, you're right."

Run di place
Example: "Di boss man run di place wid iron hand."
Translation: "The boss runs the place with a strict approach."

Rewind and come again
Example: "Di DJ seh rewind and come again, drop di tune one more time."
Translation: "The DJ said to play the song again, let's hear it one more time."

Rude gyal
Example: "Di rude gyal dem always a party pon di weekend."
Translation: "The tough girls are always partying on the weekend."

Riddim
Example: "Di riddim sick, everybody a move to di beat."
Translation: "The rhythm is great, everyone is moving to the beat."

Rough up
Example: "Di police rough up di suspect during di interrogation."
Translation: "The police roughened up the suspect during the interrogation."

Roll out
Example: "Wi ago roll out tonight, full crew inna di dance."
Translation: "We're going out tonight, the whole crew is going to the party."

Rinse out
Example: "Di DJ rinse out di track till di speaker dem buss."
Translation: "The DJ played the track so hard that the speakers blew."

Ride di riddim
Example: "Di artist ride di riddim well, pure vibes."
Translation: "The artist flowed well with the rhythm, pure vibes."

Run it back
Example: "Run it back, mi waan hear di tune again."
Translation: "Play it again, I want to hear the song again."

Real deal
Example: "Di man a di real deal, nuh fake business."
Translation: "The man is genuine, no fake business."

Run outta luck
Example: "Him run outta luck when di police catch him."
Translation: "He ran out of luck when the police caught him."

S

Settle down
Example: "Settle down, nuh mek no noise inna di place."
Translation: "Calm down, don't make any noise in the place."

Soca
Example: "Di soca music a play, di vibe nice."
Translation: "The soca music is playing, the vibe is great."

Sistren
Example: "Mi sistren an' mi always a look out fi each other."
Translation: "My female friends and I always look out for each other."

Sell off
Example: "Di party sell off last night, pure people."
Translation: "The party was amazing last night, it was packed."

Star bwoy
Example: "Di yute a di star bwoy inna di community."
Translation: "The young man is the star in the community."

Screw face
Example: "Nuh screw yuh face, di tings soon sort out."
Translation: "Don't frown, things will be sorted out soon."

Siddung
Example: "Siddung an' relax, mi wi handle it."
Translation: "Sit down and relax, I'll handle it."

Shell dung
Example: "Di artist shell dung di stage wid him performance."
Translation: "The artist rocked the stage with his performance."

Sweet like sugar
Example: "Di juice sweet like sugar, mi love it."
Translation: "The juice is very sweet, I love it."

Same way
Example: "Mi wi help yuh same way, nuh worry."
Translation: "I'll help you anyway, don't worry."

Spliff
Example: "Him a bun a spliff pon di corner."
Translation: "He's smoking a joint on the corner."

Skip town
Example: "Di man skip town after di incident."
Translation: "The man left town after the incident."

Style
Example: "Yuh always a change up yuh style, mi rate dat."
Translation: "You're always changing your style, I respect that."

Swag
Example: "Di man have pure swag, nuh ordinary."
Translation: "The man has pure style, not ordinary."

Step out

Example: "Wi a go step out tonight an' enjoy weself."
Translation: "We're going out tonight to enjoy ourselves."

Straight up
Example: "Straight up, mi nah go round di truth."
Translation: "Honestly, I'm not going to hide the truth."

Sumn fi sumn
Example: "If yuh waan mi help, is sumn fi sumn."
Translation: "If you want my help, you have to give something in return."

Sufferation
Example: "Di people dem a face nuff sufferation right now."
Translation: "The people are facing a lot of hardship right now."

Step up
Example: "Mi haffi step up mi game fi di next match."
Translation: "I have to improve my performance for the next match."

Siddung pon di ends
Example: "Mi deh yah siddung pon di ends wid mi fren dem."
Translation: "I'm here sitting around with my friends."

T

Tek time
Example: "Tek time wid di likkle pickney, nuh rush him."
Translation: "Take it easy with the little child, don't rush him."

Tallawah
Example: "She likkle but she tallawah, nuh underestimate her."
Translation: "She's small but mighty, don't underestimate her."

Tump
Example: "Him tump di ball hard inna di goal."
Translation: "He hit the ball hard into the goal."

Tek weh yuhself
Example: "Mi tell yuh fi tek weh yuhself from trouble."
Translation: "I told you to remove yourself from trouble."

Turn up di vibes
Example: "Di party lit, turn up di vibes even more."
Translation: "The party is great, increase the excitement even more."

Tumpa
Example: "Him fall an' gi di ground a tumpa."
Translation: "He fell and hit the ground hard."

Tek heed
Example: "Tek heed to di warning, nuh mek di same mistake."

Translation: "Pay attention to the warning, don't make the same mistake."

Trus mi
Example: "Trus mi, di plan gwine work."
Translation: "Trust me, the plan will work."

Talk di tings
Example: "Talk di tings dem weh really a gwaan."
Translation: "Speak about what's really happening."

Trod
Example: "Mi trod pon di path of righteousness."
Translation: "I walk on the path of righteousness."

Tuff like iron
Example: "Di man tuff like iron, nuthing cyaan beat him."
Translation: "The man is as tough as iron, nothing can defeat him."

Touch road
Example: "Wi a go touch road later fi di party."
Translation: "We're going out later for the party."

Tek it easy
Example: "Tek it easy, nuh rush di process."
Translation: "Take it easy, don't rush the process."

Trod carefully
Example: "Trod carefully, di journey rough."
Translation: "Proceed carefully, the journey is tough."

Tek charge

Example: "Yuh need fi tek charge of di situation."
Translation: "You need to take control of the situation."

Turn round
Example: "Di man turn round him life after di rough times."
Translation: "The man turned his life around after the tough times."

Tek up space
Example: "Nuh tek up space if yuh nah contribute."
Translation: "Don't take up space if you're not contributing."

Turn head
Example: "Di new girl turn everybody head inna di office."
Translation: "The new girl caught everyone's attention in the office."

Touch base
Example: "Mi wi touch base wid yuh later, mek wi talk."
Translation: "I'll get in touch with you later, let's talk."

Tek stock
Example: "Mi haffi tek stock of di situation before mi act."
Translation: "I have to assess the situation before I act."

U

Uptown
Example: "Di uptown yute dem always a flex inna di nice areas."
Translation: "The upper-class youths are always hanging out in the nice areas."

Upting
Example: "Mi a go upting di place wid mi new ride."
Translation: "I'm going to show off the place with my new car."

Undercover
Example: "Him a move undercover, nobody cyaan spot him."
Translation: "He's moving secretly, no one can spot him."

Up deh
Example: "Di man deh pon a level, him up deh fi true."
Translation: "The man is on a different level, he's truly on top."

Up to di time
Example: "Mi style up to di time, always current."
Translation: "My style is up-to-date, always current."

Under mi wings
Example: "Mi tek him under mi wings an' show him di ropes."
Translation: "I took him under my wing and showed him the way."

Up like seven
Example: "Di energy up like seven inna di dancehall."
Translation: "The energy is high in the dancehall."

Under heavy manners
Example: "Di community under heavy manners from di law."
Translation: "The community is under strict control by the law."

Upful vibes
Example: "Wi always a promote upful vibes inna di gathering."
Translation: "We always promote positive vibes in the gathering."

Uplift
Example: "Di song a uplift mi spirit everytime mi hear it."
Translation: "The song uplifts my spirit every time I hear it."

Under pressure
Example: "Di team under pressure fi win di match."
Translation: "The team is under pressure to win the match."

Up move
Example: "Mi mek a up move fi better mi life."
Translation: "I made a positive move to improve my life."

Up an' running
Example: "Di business up an' running from early morning."

Translation: "The business has been active since early morning."

Upful
Example: "Mi waan keep di vibes upful, nuh negative energy."
Translation: "I want to keep the vibes positive, no negative energy."

Up and at it
Example: "Mi up and at it, ready fi tackle di day."
Translation: "I'm up and ready, prepared to tackle the day."

Unuh
Example: "Unuh fi listen when mi a talk."
Translation: "You all need to listen when I'm speaking."

Under wraps
Example: "Di plans fi di party deh under wraps till further notice."
Translation: "The plans for the party are being kept secret for now."

Up di ting
Example: "Wi need fi up di ting if wi waan succeed."
Translation: "We need to step up our efforts if we want to succeed."

Under di radar
Example: "Him always a stay under di radar, nuh like spotlight."

Translation: "He always stays out of the spotlight, doesn't like attention."

Up inna yuh business
Example: "Dem always up inna yuh business, mind dem own!"
Translation: "They're always in your business, they should mind their own!"

V

Vex
Example: "Mi vex because dem never invite mi."
Translation: "I'm upset because they didn't invite me."

Vibes
Example: "Di vibes a di party was lit, pure enjoyment."
Translation: "The atmosphere at the party was great, pure enjoyment."

Vibes it up
Example: "Wi ago vibes it up tonight wid some good music."
Translation: "We're going to have a good time tonight with some good music."

Violate
Example: "Dem violate mi, so mi haffi defend miself."
Translation: "They disrespected me, so I had to defend myself."

Visionary
Example: "Him a visionary, always a think ahead."
Translation: "He's a visionary, always thinking ahead."

Vex money
Example: "Always keep vex money, yuh never know when yuh need fi leave."
Translation: "Always keep emergency money, you never know when you'll need to leave."

Viable
Example: "Di plan sound viable, wi fi give it a try."
Translation: "The plan seems doable, we should give it a try."

Voice
Example: "Mi a go voice mi opinion pon di matter."
Translation: "I'm going to express my opinion on the matter."

Vexation
Example: "Di whole situation bring nuff vexation to mi."
Translation: "The whole situation caused me a lot of frustration."

Vybz
Example: "Mi like di vybz of di new tune weh di DJ drop."
Translation: "I like the vibe of the new song the DJ played."

Vendetta
Example: "Dem a keep a vendetta against mi fi no reason."
Translation: "They're holding a grudge against me for no reason."

Vibes Cartel
Example: "Di man a deejay like Vibes Cartel, full a lyrics."
Translation: "The man deejays like Vybz Kartel, full of lyrics."

Valiant
Example: "Him mek a valiant effort fi win di race."
Translation: "He made a brave effort to win the race."

Viewpoint
Example: "Mi appreciate yuh viewpoint, it mek sense."
Translation: "I appreciate your perspective, it makes sense."

Vow
Example: "Mi mek a vow fi always be there fi mi family."
Translation: "I made a promise to always be there for my family."

Vanquish
Example: "Wi plan fi vanquish di competition wid our new product."
Translation: "We plan to defeat the competition with our new product."

Venture
Example: "Mi a start a new venture inna di business world."
Translation: "I'm starting a new venture in the business world."

Vivid
Example: "Mi have a vivid memory of di event."
Translation: "I have a clear memory of the event."

Vibe killer
Example: "Nuh bring no bad energy, yuh a vibe killer."
Translation: "Don't bring any bad energy, you're ruining the vibe."

W

Wah gwaan?
Example: "Wah gwaan, mi friend?"
Translation: "What's up, my friend?"

Weh yuh deh?
Example: "Weh yuh deh? Mi nuh see yuh long time."
Translation: "Where have you been? I haven't seen you in a long time."

Wicked
Example: "Di performance wicked, mi rate it."
Translation: "The performance was amazing, I really liked it."

Wull a vibes
Example: "Mi a go wull a vibes pon di beach."
Translation: "I'm going to relax and enjoy myself on the beach."

Wine up
Example: "She a wine up herself to di music."
Translation: "She's dancing seductively to the music."

Wull it dung
Example: "Mi wull it dung inna di face of adversity."
Translation: "I stayed strong in the face of adversity."

Wap dem
Example: "Di DJ wap dem wid some big tunes."

Translation: "The DJ hit them with some great tunes."

Wha yuh a seh?
Example: "Wha yuh a seh? Mi cyaan believe mi ears."
Translation: "What are you saying? I can't believe my ears."

Wap
Example: "Di man gi him a wap pon di

Wicked inna di brain
Example: "Di movie wicked inna di brain, it blow mi mind."
Translation: "The movie was mind-blowing, it blew my mind."

Wagwan
Example: "Wagwan, mi see yuh finally."
Translation: "What's going on, I finally see you."

Woss
Example: "Di new tune a woss, mi love it."
Translation: "The new song is great, I love it."

Wid di flow
Example: "Him deejay wid di flow, smooth an' cool."
Translation: "He deejays with style, smooth and cool."

Wrench up
Example: "Di tune wrench up di place, everybody a dance."
Translation: "The tune pumped up the place, everyone is dancing."

Wolley
Example: "Mi have a wolley a work fi do dis week."
Translation: "I have a lot of work to do this week."

Wicked up
Example: "Di event wicked up di whole community."
Translation: "The event made a big impact on the whole community."

Waddup
Example: "Waddup, mi fam? How yuh been?"
Translation: "What's up, my family? How have you been?"

Wit it
Example: "Him always wit it, always ready fi di action."
Translation: "He's always up for it, always ready for action."

Wile out
Example: "Di crowd wile out when di DJ start drop di hot tracks."
Translation: "The crowd went wild when the DJ started playing the hot tracks."

Wata
Example: "Di party was full a wata, everybody enjoy di night."
Translation: "The party was full of excitement, everyone enjoyed the night."

Y

Yardie
Example: "Di yardie dem have a unique style of living."
Translation: "The locals have a unique style of living."

Yuh know
Example: "Yuh know, mi always a try mi best."
Translation: "You know, I'm always trying my best."

Yute
Example: "Di yute dem a run di place."
Translation: "The youths are taking over the place."

Yam
Example: "Di yam an' saltfish a one of mi favorite dish."
Translation: "Yam and saltfish is one of my favorite dishes."

Yah so
Example: "Yah so di vibes good, pure relaxation."
Translation: "Here the vibe is good, pure relaxation."

Yamhead
Example: "Him a yamhead, always a eat yam an' nothing else."
Translation: "He's a yam-lover, always eating yam and nothing else."

Yuh see mi
Example: "Yuh see mi, mi deh yah fi di long haul."
Translation: "You see me, I'm here for the long term."

Yuh have it
Example: "Yuh have it, di skill set fi di job."
Translation: "You have it, the skill set for the job."

Yah man
Example: "Yah man, di party was wicked last night."
Translation: "Yeah man, the party was great last night."

Yawn
Example: "Di lecture was so boring mi end up a yawn."
Translation: "The lecture was so boring I ended up yawning."

Yuh must know
Example: "Yuh must know di answer to di question."
Translation: "You should know the answer to the question."

Yuh mad
Example: "Yuh mad fi think mi wi do dat?"
Translation: "Are you crazy to think I would do that?"

Yankee
Example: "Di yankee dem love di Jamaican culture."
Translation: "The Americans love Jamaican culture."

Yuh sure
Example: "Yuh sure yuh waan go through wid dat plan?"
Translation: "Are you sure you want to go through with that plan?"

Yuh self
Example: "Yuh need fi be true to yuh self."

Translation: "You need to be true to yourself."

Yea
Example: "Yea, mi get di message an' mi wi respond shortly."
Translation: "Yes, I received the message and I will respond shortly."

Yuh ready
Example: "Yuh ready fi di show? It ago be epic."
Translation: "Are you ready for the show? It's going to be epic."

Yoke
Example: "Dem a yoke up di place wid dem loud music."
Translation: "They're making noise with their loud music."

Yardie style
Example: "Di party did full a yardie style, pure fun an' vibes."
Translation: "The party was full of local style, pure fun and vibes."

Z

Zine
Example: "Mi get di information zine, mi wi follow up."
Translation: "I got the information, I'll follow up."

Zagga
Example: "Di song a zagga, it mek mi move."
Translation: "The song is energetic, it makes me move."

Zeek
Example: "Him zeek out di scene, full a style."
Translation: "He stands out in the scene, full of style."

Zeen
Example: "Yuh understand di plan? Zeen, mi get it."
Translation: "Do you understand the plan? Yes, I get it."

Zinc
Example: "Di house roof covered in zinc, it cool inside."
Translation: "The house roof is covered in zinc, it's cool inside."

Zow
Example: "Di event did zow, di vibes was high."
Translation: "The event was great, the vibe was high."

Zoot
Example: "Him roll a zoot an' chill out pon di corner."
Translation: "He rolled a joint and relaxed on the corner."

Zing

Example: "Di conversation had a lot of zing, pure excitement."
Translation: "The conversation was lively, full of excitement."

Zip it
Example: "Yuh need fi zip it an' listen to di instructions."
Translation: "You need to be quiet and listen to the instructions."

Zag
Example: "Di zig an' zag of di dance moves a impress di crowd."
Translation: "The zigzag of the dance moves is impressing the crowd."

Zoom
Example: "Di camera zoom in pon di artist while him perform."
Translation: "The camera zoomed in on the artist while he performed."

Zesty
Example: "Di food was zesty, full of flavor."
Translation: "The food was lively and full of flavor."

Zine it
Example: "Mi zine it, mi wi handle di matter."
Translation: "I got it, I'll handle the matter."

Zinc roof
Example: "Di zinc roof cool di house an' keep di rain out."

Translation: "The zinc roof keeps the house cool and keeps the rain out."

Zim
Example: "Di man inna di zim, him always on point."
Translation: "The man is in the zone, he's always on point."

Zippa
Example: "Di DJ drop a zippa tune, everybody a dance."
Translation: "The DJ dropped a hit song, everyone is dancing."

Zooted
Example: "Him get zooted an' just relax."
Translation: "He got high and just relaxed."

Zillion
Example: "Mi love di view from di top, it worth a zillion."
Translation: "I love the view from the top, it's priceless."

Zee
Example: "Yuh zee di new car mi just buy?"
Translation: "Did you see the new car I just bought?"

Zug
Example: "Di vibes a di event zug, everybody excited."
Translation: "The vibe at the event is intense, everyone is excited."

Printed in Great Britain
by Amazon

62589105R00047